Conversations with Grief

Gemma Hughes

BookLeaf Publishing

Presentation by *BookLeaf Publishing*

Web: www.bookleafpub.com

E-mail: info@bookleafpub.com

ISBN: 9789357211239

First edition 2022

DEDICATION

To you who grieve.

To you who suffer because you loved so much.

To you who cannot move on, but hope to move forward.

PREFACE

Inside my mother's coffin was a letter I had written to her. I wrote the letter on the day that my counsellor made the suggestion. It gave me a focus, and while I do remember writing it, I would not be able to recall the words. It was entirely private, a real and honest outpouring of everything I felt at the time. I remember crying as I wrote it, and feeling comfort from my belief that this was a form of communication with her. Yes, I did actually believe she would read it.

Back in 1991 I was at the beginning of a thirty-year arc, a journey yet to be travelled with grief, a travelling companion nobody would ever choose. I had very few people to talk to about the fact that I missed my mother so terribly, and so I wrote things down, mostly about her, but sometimes about other things I grieved over.

Grief has travelled with me on paper for many years, and now I am proud to have put all of these conversations into this book.

PRAED STREET

Standing in front of the iconic St Mary's Hospital arch, I ache with sorrow.

It was not my intention to be here today, I had made no plans ever to come.

This building has interrupted my return to Paddington Station

On a summer's afternoon, I was just walking home.

Now I am crushed by a weight of nostalgia.

I stand outside this building in which my mother lived, studied, and nursed.

Where she became accomplished in her profession, navigated friendships and colleague relationships, and wept over men who broke their promises.

Immobile in the presence of this great hospital, my breathing has shortened as my heart pounds.

I am overwhelmed to be standing in this same spot as she once did.

I wonder if those around me have noticed that I am lingering here a little too long.

Tears are welling in my eyes, ones I am desperate to stop from falling, to save me from my shame.

The shame I have carried for so long, that tells me I should be over all of this by now.

My eyes run along the arch from left to right, then back again.

I focus on the unusual brickwork, the deliberate mottle of browns and reds.

It's majestic gold lettering denotes that this is a place of importance, of prominence.

It would have looked just like this when she was here.

Only time is separating us, cruel, cruel time, the master of division.

Why did she have so many years without me, and I so many years without her?

Such is the way of mother and child, two lives that eclipse for a short while before they are severed, for there is no gentle way of breaking the bond.

In a span of seventy-one years from her birth to now, we shared just twelve.

I want to meet this young nurse for a coffee, listen to her plans and worries for the future, and ask her about Swinging London.

This young nurse who'd ventured here from a foreign country, with so much wonderment for what was to come.

While I with so much longing for what had been.

IN GRIEF

Grief, the silent partner,
Is matching me step for step,
As I walk through the corridors and open plains of my life.

She is reminding me with every breath,
Of all that I have lost,
Of everything which may and should have been.

At the junction,
She walks one way, and I another,
Naively free of her, I skip and laugh as though I have wings.

Her fog lifts, to leave me feeling as myself again,
I have no cares as I look forward,
To the future, to happiness.

Abruptly I feel a tug on my arm,
I had not expected her,
I was too well recovered to anticipate her visit.

I have had enough of walking with this malevolent beast,

I did not want her to return,
And now even more persistent and demanding.

I turn and run, through thickets and brambles,
Cutting through my clothes until they draw blood.
She runs faster, until I expire.

I hope my indignance at being the object of her torment
Will lessen her engagement in this battle
But it does not.

Exhausted, frustrated, empty,
With the final ounce of energy I possess
I stop, and turn to face her.

"Will you not leave me?" I plead
She shakes her head and tells me she cannot,
She is part of me, not separate.

"Join me in this moment"
She whispers to me as she takes my hands.
"There can be no more avoidance"

I walk with her,
I hold her hand,
I feel everything – the loss, the pain, the regret, the guilt.

I fall to the ground,
To the depths of my despair,
To the bottom of my loss.

I feel it fully until I reach my end,
I cry every tear until I am dry,
Finally, I can exhale.

She holds me tightly,
And tells me she is only here because I loved,
There is no escape.

She turns and walks away
I know she will return to walk with me again,
A little shorter the next time.

GOODBYE

Like the last spec of sunlight,
The last glimmer of hope,
Your nightmare has been brought to an end,
But I have not yet slept.

Your sweating brow,
My salty tears,
The purification of our bodies,
Memories from previous years.

I am relieved,
I feel guilty for that,
No more anxious waiting ahead,
Only certainty and truth.

No more worrying when or how,
My love for you is still on earth,
I hold on to a part of you,
Perhaps you have not all gone.

My grievances are worthless emotions,
This is not goodbye,
This is au-revoir,
Maybe there is more anxious waiting.

GREATEST LESSONS

For so long I felt stuck and confined by what I viewed as my own back luck.

Losing my mother at such a young age felt like an awful injustice. A pain that only I was experiencing.

As humans, we hope to get through life without any form of suffering, and I compared myself to others who appeared to have things so much easier than I.

After far too many years, I came to understand that everybody suffers, even though it may not be obvious from what they show to the outside world.

A person can appear very capable and together, and may never speak of their pain, however there are very few who remain unscathed in the world.

I no longer believe in judgement around the hierarchy of suffering because there are so many ways in which a person can experience trauma, loss, stress, bullying, neglect and exclusion.

Two people can go through the very same experience, and react in completely different ways. It is the privilege of the individual to determine their sufferings, not for those around them to decide.

I believe that despite what is taken from you, you retain your ability to choose your attitude and to choose your own way.

The human freedom to choose the outlook of my own situation was an awakening that came late to me.

It is not an easy choice to remain grateful for a life in which the loss of a loved one bears down on one's shoulders with the deepest of pain.

Yet still, it is a choice.

It was many years before I realised I could take ownership of the impact that my mother’s death would have on me.

I spent many years feeling sorry for myself, with a victim mentality. I did this to the detriment of recognising many of the good things I had.

I did not want to hear that I had the power to improve my situation.

Over time I have learned that I can tame the thought processes that keep me small, and although I don't win every day, as I am an imperfect human being, I lose less often.

I sit with my sad thoughts.

I allow myself to feel joy.

I give each of them their turn, and my full attention.

I ask them to co-exist, not cancel the other out.

OH CHRISTMAS TREE

I stared at the Christmas tree.

Decorated by the children, as they had done every year since they could walk.

The room lay still, following their departure to bed.

Lights twinkled, with memories on every bauble.

I whispered "Mum can you see it? Can you see our tree?"

"Tell me you can see it."

I waited in the stillness.

Nothing.

Just a little emptiness in the air.

The same amount of emptiness that had lingered so many times.

I wondered how something so weightless could feel so heavy.

How a lack of presence could feel so present.

I knew this moment would pass, I knew I was being sentimental, and that I was conjuring some of these dark feelings.

Feelings I was now so very good at manifesting.

They were seductive.

Be sad, you are safe in the sadness.

I turned out the lights and walked up to bed.

Just a little moment of grief.

Maybe ninety seconds in all.

And this is how it was with this little visitor and I.

Moments here and there to catch me.

Life in all of it’s normality, and then a sudden jolt.

Oh wouldn’t it be wonderful if your mother could see it.

And how could I do anything but agree?

WARM PASTRIES

I entered the flat and she wasn't there.

She was not there as I had expected her to be.

I had bought the pastries from the bakery by the station.

The ones I would always buy on my way to their flat.

Why shouldn't I buy them now?

I was excited.

Excited to see her.

But wait, she wasn't there.

I knew that she wouldn't be, didn't I?

But I still had the pastries.

The pastries were warm, just as she liked them.

She would take out the plates and the knives, some butter and jam, and we three would sit around the circular table by the window.

Eating together, all three of us.

Three.

But wait, she wasn't there.

I want her to be there in the flat, in front of me now.

The wanting should be enough!

She had always been here whenever I had visited, and so she should still be.

My father has accepted her death.

He will not talk of a meal with a visitor who will never arrive.

I wipe my eyes quickly.

I go to the kitchen and take out three plates.

I must stop this.

I put one back.

I place the two plates on the table.

I pull a pastry out of the bag and place it on my father's plate, then one for me.

There is one left in the bag.

We both look at the bag.

I am embarrassed.

Why have I bought my mother a croissant?

I am a mad woman.

She isn’t here, and yet she must be.

MISCARRIAGE

The pictures of your face,
Which I will never see,
I cannot remember,
For there are no memories.

Little hands so small,
The beating of your heart,
We never were together,
Yet we never were apart.

Thoughts plague my mind,
I sit alone and cry,
I never had the chance to say hello,
But I had to say goodbye.

What would it have been like to hold you close,
For just that one short while,
To feel the softness of your skin,
And see the innocence of your smile.

I can't expect you to understand,
As you lay there in my womb,
A perfectly formed rosebud,
Without the chance to bloom.

I only wanted to be your mother,
But I did not have the choice,
I imagine who you may have been,
Your touch, your love, your voice.

PRAYERS OF A TWELVE YEAR OLD CHILD

The twelve-year-old me who prayed to God with so much hope and desperation felt deserted.

All of the power I was told he yielded, by the figures of authority in my life, the priests, teachers and parents, seemed so completely out of reach to me.

This rejection of my prayers was a massive source of resentment long after Mum's coffin had been lowered into the ground.

It was also a source of internal conflict as my mother had brought me up in the Catholic faith, and so any desertion of those beliefs felt like the desertion of her.

Despite my questioning God, I still believed that her soul would go on, despite her body remaining on the earth plane.

The hopeful person in me believed that she had transitioned to a better place.

I wondered if communication between us and the afterlife was possible.

Sometimes I would send a question out there, and it seemed that I would receive a reply.

At other times, there was just silence.

The questioning of my faith led me to a common place, to the essence of what it was to be human.

I came to understand that I was part of a much bigger picture, connected, in a sequence where what I did to myself, I ultimately did to others.

It was not easy to remain faithful to God, with so many prayers unanswered, however, I tried.

The alternative was too dark a place to venture.

Too cold a place for my heart to go.

HIGHGATE CEMETERY

In a common grave he lies
In Highgate Cemetery
Through the West Gate
And up the winding path
He hides for me to find.

Amongst the bluebells he sits
In Highgate Cemetery
Their deepest purple hue
Outnumbered by wild garlic
Releasing its aroma as I wander in.

Rich and poor interspersed
In Highgate Cemetery
Monuments so grand
Cast wealthy shadows
Over grassy neighbours.

There is no headstone for him
In Highgate Cemetery
No words of poetry
Nor name nor date
To mark his final resting place.

I find my Grandfather
In Highgate Cemetery
Encased by trees
The choir of birdsong
And long-forgotten graves.

What a heaven I have found
In Highgate Cemetery.

FOUNDATIONS OF MOTHERING

Although thirty years is a long time to be without my mother, I do realise that everything that she filled me with, during the first twelve years of my life, didn't die.

Mothering is done in the moment, with an eye on the future.

It's an education, a foundation, and pillars on which I build myself upon.

I may not remember every conversation I had with her, in fact I can only recall fragments.

However, each time we looked into each other's eyes.

Every cuddle.

Each change of my bedsheets.

Every wash of my clothes.

Each boundary she upheld.

Every time she brushed my hair before bedtime with my soft black and orange Mason-Pearson brush.

Each bedtime prayer we said together.

Those are the foundations on which I stand.

LOOKING BACK

As I stood by the graveside and threw my handful of dirt on top of her coffin, I wanted to jump into that hole with her.

Such was my desire to be with her.

That this bond between mother and daughter could be severed so permanently was destroying me.

The world had ended as I knew it, and I didn't want to live in the motherless version.

Life after Mum was a biome of grief, sadness and despair.

I was grappling with the concept of her not being here, while my mind was full of her.

The guilt I had for the relief I experienced when she died was something that weighed heavily on me for a long time.

It was many years before I understood it to be common for loved ones to experience a sense of relief when the suffering of a loved one ended with death.

I wasn't an evil person because of it, and any relief I had felt in her suffering ending was minuscule in comparison with the pain of losing her.

When I look back on that scene by her graveside, I feel proud of that young girl.

She was so desperately trying to hold herself together. She was alone with the task of organising her emotions to make sense of them.

I wish I could travel back in time and give her a big hug to let her know that she would be okay.

Eventually, she would be okay.

ESCAPISM FROM GRIEF

I walk the tightrope of having escapism, and not escaping too much.

A conscious form of escapism is healthy for me, as long as I keep it in tandem with the realities of life.

I don't want or need to escape from my life as I once did as a younger girl.

I just need moments that are for me, where I am so absorbed by the task at hand that I experience a flow-like state.

Be that riding my horse, pruning my rose garden, or settling down to a family movie.

These moments allow me to tackle life's difficulties head-on.

I have come to learn to be grateful for the suffering that comes with life and to learn what I can from it.

Grief and suffering have been a professor like no other.

I have made peace with them, I listen to what they want to teach me, but then they must leave me alone during the in-between times.

That is the deal, my little formula to thrive in my life.

WISH

I wish you were here
Not there
Wherever there may be
Whether in heaven
On the wings of the breeze
Or solely in my memories
I wish you were here
Not there.

PAPÁ

My father is a shadow of himself as he meets old age with a solemn bow.

Deferring to his frailty in a way I wish he wouldn't.

For when we give in to it, surely then it grabs us forcefully, pulling us back to the dependence of our childhood.

He has stopped fighting, but who am I to judge him, when he has fought for so much of his life.

Fighting for the Republicans,

Fighting to survive his imprisonment,

Fighting the traumatic memories of the Spanish Civil War,

Fighting to fit back into his family after four years away,

Fighting to survive in a new country,

Fighting for employment as an old man past his prime,

Fighting his grief after the death of his beloved wife.

Why would he fight to live any longer?

He loves his grandchildren, and I wonder if this is his sole motivation.

He has no other interests, and neither does he want any.

What diversions can I use to tempt a man who worked all the hours he could, and then spent his evenings of respite in the company of his late wife?

I find this all very hard to accept, because I want him to fight for me, his daughter.

I need him in my life, and in that of my children.

This drifting away is troubling me.

42

At the age of forty-two, I face a new arc which I call my "extra time".

As I reach the age my mother was when she died, I have a new appreciation of how precious life is.

I have a new perspective of all of the things she was unable to do and how privileged I am in this moment to have my health and freedoms.

To have new experiences and to be able to look forward.

I have a strong desire to live a purposeful life that benefits others, and I want to be kinder to myself after invoking so much self-hatred for far too long.

If Mum could see me now, I know that this is all that she would want for her daughter, and it is the greatest gift I can give to her.

For what you have lost, only you know that value of.

You will survive, you will thrive, you will laugh again, you will move forwards with your life in a timescale that is yours alone.

There are no rules.

Grief is entwined with love, and love has no end.

HOLDING TIGHT

There was a time when I believed that the grief I was experiencing because of my mother's death would never loosen its hold.

It held me so tight that I was too scared to live.

In those early days when my grief was at its most intense, I felt suffocated by it.

The pain was physical, in my stomach, in my chest as though my lungs were filled with a toxic black smoke.

My relationship with my grief determined the level of energy I could put out into the world.

It clouded my thoughts, and it was my thoughts.

Many days I felt heavy, as if I were being pulled down by weights.

For a long time grief turned the lights out, and each day was survival.

It's unpleasant to look back on myself as a child and adolescent because I was so broken, disconnected and defensive.

I retreated into myself, part of me is still in that cave now, and I am not sure if I will ever coax all of her out.

I still need to give myself reminders that although I know I am able to face the world alone, sometimes it's just nicer not to.

As I look back on my journey, I realise how many times I tried to escape from what was essentially a part of my own self.

My healing began when I firmly looked grief in the face and submitted to her long enough to process my pain.

And when I realised that if I could speak my mother's name, if she was in my thoughts and in my heart, then she could not die.

STABLE DOOR

No longer over the stable door
His head there waiting for my return
With tack or feed or apple core
Oh how the empty sight makes me yearn.

No longer over the stable door
A muddy face from rolling fun
Pricked ears, and eyes that saw beyond
Our time was surely not yet done.

No longer over the stable door
Generous of spirit, and of heart
How I will treasure our memories
As though we never were apart.

No longer over the stable door
I whispered to him 'now run free'
Your spirit is your own again
You no longer belong to me.

No longer over the stable door
Dear friend I hope to meet again
In fields we'll jump and gallop too
Over fallen logs, and grassy terrain.

PLEASE

Please one more cup of tea,
One last word of advice,
Over a lemon drizzle.
Time steals you over and over again,
Each time I boil the kettle.

AFFIRMATIONS OF A MOTHERLESS DAUGHTER

I acknowledge your absence: knowing my heart is full of your love.
I remember you during important milestones in my life: understanding that you would be with me if you could.
I accept that you are not available for my children: I will ensure that they know who their grandmother is.
I can miss our conversations: and also speak to you every day.
I am grateful for everything that your death has taught me: to be resilient, empathetic, and grateful.
I take my journey with grief one step at a time: conscious that I may never move on but I hope to move forwards.
I am whole, I am enough, I am connected to you and always will be.
I send love out to the universe, and to all daughters living without their mother.

www.ingramcontent.com/pod-product-compliance
Lightning Source LLC
Chambersburg PA
CBHW051744130826
49812CB00033B/990
9789357211239